Three, Four, Get Some More

Another Ultimate Guide to Our Soles

Josée Scalabrini

Henley Point
Toronto

Copyright © 2022 Josée Scalabrini
Three, Four, Get Some More: Another Ultimate Guide to Our Soles

by Josée Scalabrini

Published by Henley Point
Toronto, Canada
www.henleypoint.ca

All rights reserved. No portion of this book may be reproduced in any form without permission from the publisher, except as permitted by copyright law in Canada and the United States of America. For permissions contact: info@henleypoint.ca.

The information contained in this publication is provided for informational and referential purposes only, and should not be construed as legal advice on any subject matter.

Neither the publisher nor the author is responsible for websites (or their content) that are not owned by the publisher or author.

Design and artwork: Henley Point Productions
ISBN: 978-1-7778-3476-0

WELCOME TO ANOTHER ULTIMATE GUIDE

I love shoes. And I love my shoe collection. I stated that in the first book, **One, Two, Buckle My Shoe Collection.**

That book was designed to be your reference manual, collection guide and personal content diary.

This book, **Three, Four, Get Some More: Another Ultimate Guide to Our Soles,** is also for shoe lovers and collectors and is the continuation of **One, Two, Buckle My Shoe Collection.** With diary entries for up to another 108 pairs, this book simplifies organization, storage and record keeping for insurance purposes.

Three, Four, Get Some More also comes with a comprehensive footwear glossary.

So you can use this book as a stand-alone entry and diary system for your shoes.

You can also use it as a continuation and accompaniment to its predecessor book, **One, Two, Buckle My Shoe Collection** – which also features a reporting system for up to 108 pairs, but also includes advice, insights and resources on cleaning, storage options, care, repair, maintenance, insurance and just about any other topic a shoe collector would find valuable.

One, Two, Buckle My Shoe Collection: The Ultimate Guide to Our Soles and **Three, Four, Get Some More: Another Ultimate Guide to Our Soles**. Individually, these books are must-have registration diaries for the passionate shoe collector. Together they make a perfect addition to any shoe lover's collection.

Josée

My Collection

Brand: _____ Colour: _____

Name: _____ Size: _____

Style: _____

Care: _____

_____

Storage: _____

_____

Story, fun fact: _____

_____

_____

Purchase date: _____ Price: _____

Brand: _____ Colour: _____

Name: _____ Size: _____

Style: _____

Care: _____

_____

Storage: _____

_____

Story, fun fact: _____

_____

_____

Purchase date: _____ Price: _____

Brand: _____ Colour: _____

Name: _____ Size: _____

Style: _____

Care: _____

_____

Storage: _____

_____

Story, fun fact: _____

_____

_____

Purchase date: _____ Price: _____

Brand: _____ Colour: _____

Name: _____ Size: _____

Style: _____

Care: _____

_____

Storage: _____

_____

Story, fun fact: _____

_____

_____

Purchase date: _____ Price: _____

Brand: _____ Colour: _____

Name: _____ Size: _____

Style: _____

Care: _____

_____

Storage: _____

_____

Story, fun fact: _____

_____

_____

Purchase date: _____ Price: _____

Brand: _____   Colour: _____

Name: _____   Size: _____

Style: _____

Care: _____

_____

Storage: _____

_____

Story, fun fact: _____

_____

_____

Purchase date: _____   Price: _____

My collection

Photo here

Brand: _____ Colour: _____

Name: _____ Size: _____

Style: _____

Care: _____

_____

Storage: _____

_____

Story, fun fact: _____

_____

_____

Purchase date: _____ Price: _____

Brand:_____   Colour:_____

Name: _____   Size:_____

Style:_____

Care:_____

_____

Storage:_____

_____

Story, fun fact:_____

_____

_____

Purchase date:_____   Price:_____

Brand: _____   Colour: _____

Name: _____   Size: _____

Style: _____

Care: _____

_____

Storage: _____

_____

Story, fun fact: _____

_____

_____

Purchase date: _____   Price: _____

Brand: _____ Colour: _____

Name: _____ Size: _____

Style: _____

Care: _____

_____

Storage: _____

_____

Story, fun fact: _____

_____

_____

Purchase date: _____ Price: _____

Brand: _____ Colour: _____

Name: _____ Size: _____

Style: _____

Care: _____

_____

Storage: _____

_____

Story, fun fact: _____

_____

_____

Purchase date: _____ Price: _____

Brand:_____ Colour:_____

Name: _____ Size:_____

Style:_____

Care:_____

_____

Storage:_____

_____

Story, fun fact:_____

_____

_____

Purchase date:_____ Price:_____

Brand: _____ Colour: _____

Name: _____ Size: _____

Style: _____

Care: _____

_____

Storage: _____

_____

Story, fun fact: _____

_____

_____

Purchase date: _____ Price: _____

Brand: _____ Colour: _____

Name: _____ Size: _____

Style: _____

Care: _____

_____

Storage: _____

_____

Story, fun fact: _____

_____

_____

Purchase date: _____ Price: _____

Brand: _____ Colour: _____

Name: _____ Size: _____

Style: _____

Care: _____

_____

Storage: _____

_____

Story, fun fact: _____

_____

_____

Purchase date: _____ Price: _____

Brand:_____ Colour:_____

Name: _____ Size:_____

Style:_____

Care:_____

_____

Storage:_____

_____

Story, fun fact:_____

_____

_____

Purchase date:_____ Price:_____

Brand: _____ Colour: _____

Name: _____ Size: _____

Style: _____

Care: _____

_____

Storage: _____

_____

Story, fun fact: _____

_____

_____

Purchase date: _____ Price: _____

Brand: _____   Colour: _____

Name: _____   Size: _____

Style: _____

Care: _____
_____

Storage: _____
_____

Story, fun fact: _____
_____
_____

Purchase date: _____   Price: _____

Brand: _____   Colour: _____
Name: _____   Size: _____
Style: _____
Care: _____
_____
Storage: _____
_____
Story, fun fact: _____
_____
_____
Purchase date: _____   Price: _____

Brand: _____ Colour: _____

Name: _____ Size: _____

Style: _____

Care: _____

_____

Storage: _____

_____

Story, fun fact: _____

_____

_____

Purchase date: _____ Price: _____

Brand: _____ Colour: _____

Name: _____ Size: _____

Style: _____

Care: _____

_____

Storage: _____

_____

Story, fun fact: _____

_____

_____

Purchase date: _____ Price: _____

Brand: _____ Colour: _____

Name: _____ Size: _____

Style: _____

Care: _____
_____

Storage: _____
_____

Story, fun fact: _____
_____
_____

Purchase date: _____ Price: _____

Brand: _____ Colour: _____

Name: _____ Size: _____

Style: _____

Care: _____

_____

Storage: _____

_____

Story, fun fact: _____

_____

_____

Purchase date: _____ Price: _____

Brand:_____ Colour:_____

Name:_____ Size:_____

Style:_____

Care:_____

_____

Storage:_____

_____

Story, fun fact:_____

_____

_____

Purchase date:_____ Price:_____

Brand:_____ Colour:_____

Name:_____ Size:_____

Style:_____

Care:_____
_____

Storage:_____
_____

Story, fun fact:_____
_____
_____

Purchase date:_____ Price:_____

Brand: _____ Colour: _____

Name: _____ Size: _____

Style: _____

Care: _____

_____

Storage: _____

_____

Story, fun fact: _____

_____

_____

Purchase date: _____ Price: _____

My collection

Photo here

Brand: _____ Colour: _____

Name: _____ Size: _____

Style: _____

Care: _____

_____

Storage: _____

_____

Story, fun fact: _____

_____

_____

Purchase date: _____ Price: _____

My collection

Photo here

Brand:_____   Colour:_____

Name: _____   Size:_____

Style:_____

Care:_____
_____

Storage:_____
_____

Story, fun fact:_____
_____
_____

Purchase date:_____   Price:_____

Brand: _____ Colour: _____

Name: _____ Size: _____

Style: _____

Care: _____

_____

Storage: _____

_____

Story, fun fact: _____

_____

_____

Purchase date: _____ Price: _____

My collection

Photo here

Brand: _____   Colour: _____

Name: _____   Size: _____

Style: _____

Care: _____
_____

Storage: _____
_____

Story, fun fact: _____
_____
_____

Purchase date: _____   Price: _____

Brand:_____ Colour:_____

Name:_____ Size:_____

Style:_____

Care:_____

_____

Storage:_____

_____

Story, fun fact:_____

_____

_____

Purchase date:_____ Price:_____

Brand: _____   Colour: _____

Name: _____   Size: _____

Style: _____

Care: _____
_____

Storage: _____
_____

Story, fun fact: _____
_____
_____

Purchase date: _____   Price: _____

Brand: _____   Colour: _____

Name: _____   Size: _____

Style: _____

Care: _____
_____

Storage: _____
_____

Story, fun fact: _____
_____
_____

Purchase date: _____   Price: _____

Brand: _____ Colour: _____

Name: _____ Size: _____

Style: _____

Care: _____
_____

Storage: _____
_____

Story, fun fact: _____
_____
_____

Purchase date: _____ Price: _____

Brand:_____   Colour:_____

Name:_____   Size:_____

Style:_____

Care:_____

_____

Storage:_____

_____

Story, fun fact:_____

_____

_____

Purchase date:_____   Price:_____

Brand: _____   Colour: _____

Name: _____   Size: _____

Style: _____

Care: _____

_____

Storage: _____

_____

Story, fun fact: _____

_____

_____

Purchase date: _____   Price: _____

Brand:_____ Colour:_____

Name:_____ Size:_____

Style:_____

Care:_____

_____

Storage:_____

_____

Story, fun fact:_____

_____

_____

Purchase date:_____ Price:_____

Brand: _____ Colour: _____

Name: _____ Size: _____

Style: _____

Care: _____
_____

Storage: _____
_____

Story, fun fact: _____
_____
_____

Purchase date: _____ Price: _____

Brand:_____ Colour:_____

Name:_____ Size:_____

Style:_____

Care:_____

_____

Storage:_____

_____

Story, fun fact:_____

_____

_____

Purchase date:_____ Price:_____

Brand:_____ Colour:_____

Name: _____ Size:_____

Style:_____

Care:_____

_____

Storage:_____

_____

Story, fun fact:_____

_____

_____

Purchase date:_____ Price:_____

Brand: _____ Colour: _____

Name: _____ Size: _____

Style: _____

Care: _____

_____

Storage: _____

_____

Story, fun fact: _____

_____

_____

Purchase date: _____ Price: _____

My collection

Brand: _____   Colour: _____

Name: _____   Size: _____

Style: _____

Care: _____

_____

Storage: _____

_____

Story, fun fact: _____

_____

_____

Purchase date: _____   Price: _____

Brand:_____ Colour:_____

Name:_____ Size:_____

Style:_____

Care:_____

_____

Storage:_____

_____

Story, fun fact:_____

_____

_____

Purchase date:_____ Price:_____

Brand: _____ Colour: _____

Name: _____ Size: _____

Style: _____

Care: _____

_____

Storage: _____

_____

Story, fun fact: _____

_____

_____

Purchase date: _____ Price: _____

Brand: _____ Colour: _____

Name: _____ Size: _____

Style: _____

Care: _____
_____

Storage: _____
_____

Story, fun fact: _____
_____
_____

Purchase date: _____ Price: _____

Brand: _____ Colour: _____

Name: _____ Size: _____

Style: _____

Care: _____

_____

Storage: _____

_____

Story, fun fact: _____

_____

_____

Purchase date: _____ Price: _____

Brand: _____ Colour: _____

Name: _____ Size: _____

Style: _____

Care: _____

_____

Storage: _____

_____

Story, fun fact: _____

_____

_____

Purchase date: _____ Price: _____

Brand: _____ Colour: _____

Name: _____ Size: _____

Style: _____

Care: _____

_____

Storage: _____

_____

Story, fun fact: _____

_____

_____

Purchase date: _____ Price: _____

Brand: _____ Colour: _____

Name: _____ Size: _____

Style: _____

Care: _____

_____

Storage: _____

_____

Story, fun fact: _____

_____

_____

Purchase date: _____ Price: _____

Brand: _____ Colour: _____

Name: _____ Size: _____

Style: _____

Care: _____

_____

Storage: _____

_____

Story, fun fact: _____

_____

_____

Purchase date: _____ Price: _____

Brand:_____ Colour:_____

Name:_____ Size:_____

Style:_____

Care:_____

_____

Storage:_____

_____

Story, fun fact:_____

_____

_____

Purchase date:_____ Price:_____

Brand: _____ Colour: _____

Name: _____ Size: _____

Style: _____

Care: _____
_____

Storage: _____
_____

Story, fun fact: _____
_____
_____

Purchase date: _____ Price: _____

Brand: _____ Colour: _____

Name: _____ Size: _____

Style: _____

Care: _____

_____

Storage: _____

_____

Story, fun fact: _____

_____

_____

Purchase date: _____ Price: _____

My collection

Brand: _____ Colour: _____

Name: _____ Size: _____

Style: _____

Care: _____
_____

Storage: _____
_____

Story, fun fact: _____
_____
_____

Purchase date: _____ Price: _____

My collection

Photo here

Brand: _____ Colour: _____

Name: _____ Size: _____

Style: _____

Care: _____

_____

Storage: _____

_____

Story, fun fact: _____

_____

_____

Purchase date: _____ Price: _____

Brand:_____   Colour:_____

Name: _____   Size:_____

Style:_____

Care:_____

_____

Storage:_____

_____

Story, fun fact:_____

_____

_____

Purchase date:_____   Price:_____

Brand: _____ Colour: _____

Name: _____ Size: _____

Style: _____

Care: _____

Storage: _____
_____

Story, fun fact: _____
_____
_____

Purchase date: _____ Price: _____

Brand:_____ Colour:_____

Name:_____ Size:_____

Style:_____

Care:_____

_____

Storage:_____

_____

Story, fun fact:_____

_____

_____

Purchase date:_____ Price:_____

Brand: _____   Colour: _____

Name: _____   Size: _____

Style: _____

Care: _____

_____

Storage: _____

_____

Story, fun fact: _____

_____

_____

Purchase date: _____   Price: _____

Brand: _____ Colour: _____

Name: _____ Size: _____

Style: _____

Care: _____

_____

Storage: _____

_____

Story, fun fact: _____

_____

_____

Purchase date: _____ Price: _____

Brand: _____ Colour: _____

Name: _____ Size: _____

Style: _____

Care: _____

_____

Storage: _____

_____

Story, fun fact: _____

_____

_____

Purchase date: _____ Price: _____

Brand:_____ Colour:_____

Name:_____ Size:_____

Style:_____

Care:_____

_____

Storage:_____

_____

Story, fun fact:_____

_____

_____

Purchase date:_____ Price:_____

Brand:_____ Colour:_____

Name:_____ Size:_____

Style:_____

Care:_____

_____

Storage:_____

_____

Story, fun fact:_____

_____

_____

Purchase date:_____ Price:_____

Brand: _____ Colour: _____

Name: _____ Size: _____

Style: _____

Care: _____

_____

Storage: _____

_____

Story, fun fact: _____

_____

_____

Purchase date: _____ Price: _____

Brand: _____ Colour: _____

Name: _____ Size: _____

Style: _____

Care: _____

_____

Storage: _____

_____

Story, fun fact: _____

_____

_____

Purchase date: _____ Price: _____

My collection

Brand: _____ Colour: _____
Name: _____ Size: _____
Style: _____
Care: _____
_____
Storage: _____
_____
Story, fun fact: _____
_____
_____

Purchase date: _____ Price: _____

Brand: _____   Colour: _____

Name: _____   Size: _____

Style: _____

Care: _____

_____

Storage: _____

_____

Story, fun fact: _____

_____

_____

Purchase date: _____   Price: _____

Brand:_____   Colour:_____

Name: _____   Size:_____

Style:_____

Care:_____

_____

Storage:_____

_____

Story, fun fact:_____

_____

_____

Purchase date:_____   Price:_____

Brand: _____ Colour: _____

Name: _____ Size: _____

Style: _____

Care: _____

Storage: _____

Story, fun fact: _____

Purchase date: _____ Price: _____

Brand:_____ Colour:_____

Name:_____ Size:_____

Style:_____

Care:_____
_____

Storage:_____
_____

Story, fun fact:_____
_____
_____

Purchase date:_____ Price:_____

Brand:_____ Colour:_____

Name:_____ Size:_____

Style:_____

Care:_____

_____

Storage:_____

_____

Story, fun fact:_____

_____

_____

Purchase date:_____ Price:_____

Brand:_____ Colour:_____

Name:_____ Size:_____

Style:_____

Care:_____

_____

Storage:_____

_____

Story, fun fact:_____

_____

_____

Purchase date:_____ Price:_____

Brand:_____ Colour:_____

Name:_____ Size:_____

Style:_____

Care:_____

_____

Storage:_____

_____

Story, fun fact:_____

_____

_____

Purchase date:_____ Price:_____

Brand:_____ Colour:_____

Name: _____ Size:_____

Style:_____

Care:_____

_____

Storage:_____

_____

Story, fun fact:_____

_____

_____

Purchase date:_____ Price:_____

Brand: _____ Colour: _____

Name: _____ Size: _____

Style: _____

Care: _____

_____

Storage: _____

_____

Story, fun fact: _____

_____

_____

Purchase date: _____ Price: _____

Brand: _____   Colour: _____

Name: _____   Size: _____

Style: _____

Care: _____
_____

Storage: _____
_____

Story, fun fact: _____
_____
_____

Purchase date: _____   Price: _____

Brand: _____   Colour: _____

Name: _____   Size: _____

Style: _____

Care: _____
_____

Storage: _____
_____

Story, fun fact: _____
_____
_____

Purchase date: _____   Price: _____

Brand: _____ Colour: _____

Name: _____ Size: _____

Style: _____

Care: _____

_____

Storage: _____

_____

Story, fun fact: _____

_____

_____

Purchase date: _____ Price: _____

Brand: _____ Colour: _____

Name: _____ Size: _____

Style: _____

Care: _____

_____

Storage: _____

_____

Story, fun fact: _____

_____

_____

Purchase date: _____ Price: _____

Brand: _____   Colour: _____

Name: _____   Size: _____

Style: _____

Care: _____
_____

Storage: _____
_____

Story, fun fact: _____
_____
_____

Purchase date: _____   Price: _____

Brand: _____   Colour: _____

Name: _____   Size: _____

Style: _____

Care: _____

_____

Storage: _____

_____

Story, fun fact: _____

_____

_____

Purchase date: _____   Price: _____

Brand: _____ Colour: _____

Name: _____ Size: _____

Style: _____

Care: _____
_____

Storage: _____
_____

Story, fun fact: _____
_____
_____

Purchase date: _____ Price: _____

Brand: _____ Colour: _____

Name: _____ Size: _____

Style: _____

Care: _____

_____

Storage: _____

_____

Story, fun fact: _____

_____

_____

Purchase date: _____ Price: _____

Brand: _____   Colour: _____
Name: _____   Size: _____
Style: _____
Care: _____
_____
Storage: _____
_____
Story, fun fact: _____
_____
_____
Purchase date: _____   Price: _____

Brand: _____ Colour: _____

Name: _____ Size: _____

Style: _____

Care: _____

_____

Storage: _____

_____

Story, fun fact: _____

_____

_____

Purchase date: _____ Price: _____

Brand: _____ Colour: _____

Name: _____ Size: _____

Style: _____

Care: _____

_____

Storage: _____

_____

Story, fun fact: _____

_____

_____

Purchase date: _____ Price: _____

Brand: _____ Colour: _____

Name: _____ Size: _____

Style: _____

Care: _____

_____

Storage: _____

_____

Story, fun fact: _____

_____

_____

Purchase date: _____ Price: _____

My collection

Photo here

Brand:_____   Colour:_____

Name: _____   Size:_____

Style:_____

Care:_____

_____

Storage:_____

_____

Story, fun fact:_____

_____

_____

Purchase date:_____   Price:_____

Brand: _____ Colour: _____

Name: _____ Size: _____

Style: _____

Care: _____

_____

Storage: _____

_____

Story, fun fact: _____

_____

_____

Purchase date: _____ Price: _____

My collection

Brand: _____ Colour: _____

Name: _____ Size: _____

Style: _____

Care: _____
_____
_____

Storage: _____
_____
_____

Story, fun fact: _____
_____
_____
_____

Purchase date: _____ Price: _____

Brand:_____ Colour:_____

Name:_____ Size:_____

Style:_____

Care:_____

_____

Storage:_____

_____

Story, fun fact:_____

_____

_____

Purchase date:_____ Price:_____

Brand: _____ Colour: _____

Name: _____ Size: _____

Style: _____

Care: _____

_____

Storage: _____

_____

Story, fun fact: _____

_____

_____

Purchase date: _____ Price: _____

Brand: _____   Colour: _____

Name: _____   Size: _____

Style: _____

Care: _____
_____

Storage: _____
_____

Story, fun fact: _____
_____
_____

Purchase date: _____   Price: _____

Brand:_____ Colour:_____

Name:_____ Size:_____

Style:_____

Care:_____
_____

Storage:_____
_____

Story, fun fact:_____
_____
_____

Purchase date:_____ Price:_____

Brand: _____ Colour: _____

Name: _____ Size: _____

Style: _____

Care: _____

_____

Storage: _____

_____

Story, fun fact: _____

_____

_____

Purchase date: _____ Price: _____

Brand: _____   Colour: _____

Name: _____   Size: _____

Style: _____

Care: _____

_____

Storage: _____

_____

Story, fun fact: _____

_____

_____

Purchase date: _____   Price: _____

Brand: _____ Colour: _____

Name: _____ Size: _____

Style: _____

Care: _____

_____

Storage: _____

_____

Story, fun fact: _____

_____

_____

Purchase date: _____ Price: _____

Brand: _____ Colour: _____

Name: _____ Size: _____

Style: _____

Care: _____

_____

Storage: _____

_____

Story, fun fact: _____

_____

_____

Purchase date: _____ Price: _____

Brand: _____ Colour: _____

Name: _____ Size: _____

Style: _____

Care: _____

_____

Storage: _____

_____

Story, fun fact: _____

_____

_____

Purchase date: _____ Price: _____

Brand: _____ Colour: _____

Name: _____ Size: _____

Style: _____

Care: _____

_____

Storage: _____

_____

Story, fun fact: _____

_____

_____

Purchase date: _____ Price: _____

Brand: _____ Colour: _____

Name: _____ Size: _____

Style: _____

Care: _____

_____

Storage: _____

_____

Story, fun fact: _____

_____

_____

Purchase date: _____ Price: _____

My collection

Brand: _____ Colour: _____

Name: _____ Size: _____

Style: _____

Care: _____

_____

Storage: _____

_____

Story, fun fact: _____

_____

_____

Purchase date: _____ Price: _____

Brand: _____   Colour: _____

Name: _____   Size: _____

Style: _____

Care: _____

_____

Storage: _____

_____

Story, fun fact: _____

_____

_____

Purchase date: _____   Price: _____

Brand:_____   Colour:_____

Name:_____   Size:_____

Style:_____

Care:_____
_____

Storage:_____
_____

Story, fun fact:_____
_____
_____

Purchase date:_____ Price:_____

Brand: _____   Colour: _____

Name: _____   Size: _____

Style: _____

Care: _____

Storage: _____

_____

Story, fun fact: _____

_____

_____

Purchase date: _____   Price: _____

Brand: _____ Colour: _____

Name: _____ Size: _____

Style: _____

Care: _____

_____

Storage: _____

_____

Story, fun fact: _____

_____

_____

Purchase date: _____ Price: _____

Brand:_____ Colour:_____

Name:_____ Size:_____

Style:_____

Care:_____

_____

Storage:_____

_____

Story, fun fact:_____

_____

_____

Purchase date:_____ Price:_____

Brand:_____ Colour:_____

Name: _____ Size:_____

Style:_____

Care:_____

_____

Storage:_____

_____

Story, fun fact:_____

_____

_____

Purchase date:_____ Price:_____

GLOSSARY

Aglet

This is the metal or plastic tag at the end of a shoelace. The aglet makes lacing easier and it protects functional.

Algonquin Toe

Named after the Algonquin indigenous peoples, after whom the design is accredited and designed in the eighteenth century, the "Algonquin Toe" (also referred to as the Split Toe) is constructed by joining two pieces of leather together at the "vamp" and "welt" of the shoe.

Apron Toe

The Apron toe is recognized by the visible edges or stitching that finishes the toe, forming a pattern that resembles an apron along the front of the shoe.

Arch

This is the high, curved part of the sole of the foot, located between the ball of the foot and the heel. Arch also refers to the raised area of the insole of the shoe.

Ball

This is the padded area of the foot between the big toe and the arch of the foot.

Balmorals (Also known as Oxfords)

Balmorals (or "Bals") are typically ankle-high, front-laced shoes, in which the bottom of the shoe's lacing is sewn to the front of the shoe's throat, thus creating a closed "V" shape at the bottom of the lacing. When tied, the Balmoral's tongue is completely concealed, except for its tip. Folklore informs that this style received its name and popularity after Prince Albert was seen wearing such a shoe during an extended holiday at the Balmoral castle.

Bespoke

A bespoke shoe is made on a "last" that has been custom-made for an individual, rather than one of the standard lasts that used for nearly all other shoes produced. The customer of a bespoke shoe may select nearly every detail of construction.

Bicycle Toe

This is a type of toe characterized by two stitched straight line accents. The name derives from the similarity to the detailing on professional bicycling shoes.

Blake Stitched

In a shoe that is Blake stitched, the sole is attached directly to the upper of the shoe, rather than to an intermediary welt. This makes for a lightweight shoe with the sole thinner and more flexible.

Blucher (Also known as Derby or Gibson)

This is a shoe with two side panels, or "quarters", which are laced together over the tongue. The lacing is "open-throat", and allows for more adjustment or "give" around the instep than "closed-throat" Oxford "V"-shaped lacing.

Boat Shoe

This is a type of shoe originally meant to be worn aboard a boat, usually with a non-slip outsole, usually featuring side lacing details, almost always a casual shoe you can wear with or without socks.

Boot

A boot is any shoe that comes above the ankle. Boots can be formal or casual, and are often utilitarian in their design. Boots are commonly associated with certain trades or leisure activity (such as construction boots or motorcycle boots).

Brogue (Also known as Wingtips)

A Brogue is a "heavy" Balmoral, or oxford-style shoe, featured by ample 'pinking' (perforations or zig-zag detailing) and "perforations" in order to accentuate the look of the shoe's seams.

Buckle

This is a clasp at the end of a length of fabric or leather that joins one end of the material to the other.

Cap Toe

This is a type of toe style with a full toe overlay and a straight stitching line across the top part of the toe. Cap toes are typical of dress shoes

Chelsea Boot

This is a type of boot, normally ankle height, in a pull-on style with elastic side panels, or double-gore construction.

Chopines

These were very tall platform shoes, initially created to keep the feet of elite members of society protected and elevated from the dirt and mud at the street level.

Chukka Boot

This is a boot style with laces, usually with a plain toe, and is the height of the ankle.

Clog

Traditionally fashioned from wood, a clog is a footwear style featuring a closed toe, open back and a platform sole.

Cobbler

A shoe cobbler is a person who mends and repairs shoes, whereas shoemakers – or cordwainers – make the shoes from new leather. At one time, shoemakers/cordwainers were the skilled artisans tasked with making shoes out of brand-new leather, while cobblers were the ones who repaired shoes. In fact, cobblers were forbidden from working with new leather and had to use old leather for their repairs. Today, the terms are often interchangeable.

Collar

This refers to the material sewn into the opening, or the topline, of the shoe. The collar can be padded to provide increased support or comfort.

Cordwainer

This is the skilled artisan tasked with making shoes from new leather. See Cobbler for the distinction between and shoemaker and the artisan who mends shoes using old leather.

Demi Boot

This is a style of boot whose shaft is generally no taller than the anklebone.

Derby (Also known as Blucher or Gibson)

A Derby is a shoe with two side panels or "quarters" that are laced together over the tongue. The lacing is "open-throat", and allows for more adjustment or "give" around the instep than "closed-throat" Oxford "V"-shaped lacing.

Driving Moc

This is a type of casual moccasin or slip-on ideal for driving, with a flexible, pedal-gripping sole, and a wraparound protected heel.

Engineer Boot

Originally worn by the Army Corps of Engineers, this is a work-style pull-on boot characterized by instep and top straps

Espadrille

This refers to a shoe or sandal style that has a woven rope or similar material covering the wedge or sole.

Eyelet

This is the hole through which a lace is threaded. Eyelets may be reinforced with a metal ring or grommet.

Flip-Flop

This is a thong sandal with a lightweight foam outsole that makes a "flip-flop" sound when walking.

Footbed

This is the insole of the shoe, where the foot rests. Footbed is another term for insole.

Foxing

Foxing refers to a strip of rubber joining the upper and sole of a shoe. This is typically found on canvas sneakers.

Full Grain Leather

This is leather that has been tanned so that the natural texture, or grain, of the animal skin is visible.

Gentlemen's Corner

On some shoes the inner forward point of the heel is chiselled off, a feature known as a "gentleman's corner", which is intended to alleviate the problem of the points of the heels catching the bottom of pants.

Ghillie

Pronounced "gil-ee", this is a style of footwear in which the laces pass through fabric or leather rings or loops attached to the front opening of the shoe, rather than eyelets.

Gibson (Also known as Derby or Blucher)

A shoe with two side panels or "quarters" that are laced together over the tongue. The lacing is "open-throat" and allows for more adjustment or "give" around the instep than "closed-throat" Oxford "V"-shaped lacing.

Gimping (Also known as Pinking)

This term refers to the zig-zag, saw-toothed finish found the edge (or seams) of some shoes' components (particularly the toe).

Heel

The heel is the bottom-rear part of a shoe. Its function is to support the heel of the foot. Heels are often made of the same material as the sole of the shoe. A heel can be high for fashion, to make the person look taller, or flat for more comfortable use. The heel is also used to improve the balance of the shoe, increase the height of the wearer, alter posture or other decorative purposes. Sometimes raised, the high-heel is common to a form of shoe often worn by women, but sometimes by men, too.

The heel can refer to both the rear, padded area of the underside of the foot, as well as the solid part of a shoe that supports the heel cup. Standard measures for heel heights are customarily as follows: Low Heel, which is an 8/8, 1 inch high; a Medium Heel, a 16/8, 2 inches high; and a High Heel, a 24/8, is 3 inches high.

Types of shoe heels include:

> Baby Louis - The same shape as a Louis heel but a 12/8 or shorter.
>
> Built Heel - Created from layers of leather or fiber with contrasting tones.
>
> Continental - A higher heel with a slightly curved back and flat front.
>
> Cuban - A thick, stacked heel with little or no curvature and tapered at the bottom; usually medium in height.
>
> Louis Heel - Developed in the seventeenth century, it is a heel fashioned from an extension of the shoe's sole.

- Louis or French - Features a curved back and ranges in height from 16/8 to 24/8.

- Stacked - Similar to the built heel but typically can be created from synthetic and leather materials. Often found on spectator shoes.

- Wedge - A heel of any height that is as wide as the shoe itself and follows the shoe's contour from toe to heel.

Heel Seat

This is the part of the shoe situated directly below the area where the heel of the foot rests, and where the sole and the heel are joined together.

Heel Spurs

Heel spurs are soft deposits of calcium that grow on the "plantar fascia", a band of tissue that runs along the bottom of the foot, and are typically very painful.

Insert

This is a removable foot orthosis, insole or inner sole, and it accomplishes many purposes, including daily wear comfort; height enhancement; plantar fasciitis treatment; arch support; foot and joint pain relief from arthritis; leg length discrepancy; and other causes related to orthopedic correction and athletic performance.

Insole

The insole is the interior bottom of a shoe, which sits directly beneath the foot under the "footbed" (which is also known as "sock liner"). The purpose of the insole is to attach to the lasting margin of the "upper", which is wrapped around the last during the closing of the shoe during the lasting operation. Insoles are usually made of cellulosic paper board or synthetic non-woven insole board. Many shoes have removable and replaceable footbeds. Extra cushioning is often added for comfort (to control the shape, moisture, or smell of the shoe) or health reasons (to help deal with differences in the natural shape of the foot or positioning of the foot during standing or walking).

Instep

This is the area of the foot between the toes and the ankle, or the top front part of a shoe.

Jodhpur Boots

Jodhpurs are low-cut boots used primarily for equestrian activities. These may be laced or a made in a twin gore pull-on style.

Kiltie

This is a decorative, fringed tongue over the vamp of a shoe.

Lapped Seam

A lapped seam is created when two pieces of material are attached by being sewn together, one on top of the other.

Last

This is the wooden block around which the shoe is formed. The last represents the shape and size of the intended wearer's foot. Lasts can be standard sizes or bespoke.

Lasting

This refers to the process of pulling and shaping a shoe on a last.

Lift

This is one of the several layers of leather, or leather-board, used to make a heel.

Loafers (Also known as Moccasin)

Loafers are slip-on shoes noted for their comfort. The shoe's construction tends to be simple and "roomy". Another identifying feature of loafers is that they are constructed completely without fasteners.

Medial

The medial is the part of the shoe closest to a person's centre of symmetry, and the lateral is on the opposite side, away from their centre of symmetry. Most shoes have shoelaces on the upper, connecting the medial and lateral parts after one puts their shoes on and aiding in keeping their shoes on their feet.

Midsole

The midsole is the layer between the outsole and the insole, typically present for shock absorption. Some types of shoes, like running shoes, have additional material for shock absorption, usually beneath the heel of the foot, where one puts the most pressure down. Some shoes may not have a midsole at all.

Moccasin

This construction was developed from the methods used by North American indigenous peoples. A moccasin construction produces a very light, flexible and comfortable shoe with a distinctive appearance. A "bag" of leather is formed by hand stitching an apron to a vamp. This bag is dampened and then forced on to the last to form the shape of the shoe. The sole is then stitched or glued to the formed upper part. Because the soft leather goes round the foot, forming a flexible and adaptable 'bag' a moccasin is a exceptionally comfortable.

Mule

A mule is a closed-toe shoe with no back.

Nubuck

This refers to a grain leather that has been slightly brushed on the surface to create a very fine velvet-like appearance.

Orthotic

This refers to an orthopedic insole designed to cushion and stabilize the foot.

Outsole

The outsole is the layer in direct contact with the ground. Dress shoes often have leather or resin rubber outsoles; casual or work-oriented shoes have outsoles made of natural rubber or a synthetic material like polyurethane. The outsole may comprise a single piece or may be an assembly of separate pieces, often of different materials. On some shoes, the heel of the sole has a rubber plate for durability and traction, while the front is leather for style. Specialized shoes will often have modifications on this design: athletic or so-called cleated shoes like soccer, rugby, baseball and golf shoes have spikes embedded in the outsole to improve traction.

Oxford (Also known as Balmoral)

Oxfords are a style of shoe where the two flaps of leather with the piercings for the laces ("quarters") are stitched together at the bottom underneath the vamp. The laced area opens in a closed-throat "V"-shape and does not allow as much adjustment or "give" around the instep as the alternative open-throat Derby style.

Patent Leather

Patent leather is a fine grain leather is specially treated with polyurethane to create an exceptionally glossy finish, especially suitable for evening wear. Patent leather can also be used in conjunction with other leather to produce eye catching results.

Pebbled Grain

This refers to the distinctive appearance achieved with an embossed-leather grain finish that resembles a pebble surface.

Penny Loafer

This is a slip-on style shoe with a slit over the instep where a penny traditionally was placed for good luck.

Pinking (Also known as Gimping)

This term refers to the zig-zag, saw-toothed finish found the edge (or seams) of some shoes' components (particularly the toe).

Piping

This is a decorative, narrow strip of leather that typically follows the seam of a shoe.

Platform Shoe

This is a style of shoe featuring a thicker sole at the front; the heel is typically high to accommodate the higher height of the sole.

Pull Grain Leather

This refers to a natural process to temper the hide using river stones. The result is a leather with an irregular grain that's soft to the touch and flexible.

Rim

A rim is the part of the shoe where the foot enters. Another term for collar or top line.

Saddle Shoes

These are shoes with a contrast coloured instep overlay or "saddle", usually found on golf shoes or retro styles.

Sandal

This is a form of footwear with an open toe and open back that is held to the foot by strips of leather or fabric.

Scotch Grain

This refers to the embossing of leather to create a heavy, pebbled look.

Shoe Sizes

A variation between full sizes is one-third of an inch, while the difference between half sizes is one-sixth of an inch.

Shoe Width

The width of a shoe is typically measured in letters (AAA, AA, A, B, C, D, E, EE, EEE, EEEE) and refers to the width of the shoe last as measured at the ball of the foot. Widths are defined in increments of an eighth (1/8) of an inch.

Slide

A shoe featuring an open toe and open back with a band across the toe. Slides can be flat, mid-heel or high-heeled.

Sneaker

This is an athletic shoe, typically made of canvas with a rubber sole. The term "sneaker" derives comes from the wearer's ability to walk in the shoe without making noise, thus "sneaking".

Snip Toe

This is a type of toe that is tapered, with a squared front as if "snipped".

Sole

The sole is at the bottom of a shoe to make contact with the ground. Soles can be made from a variety of materials, although most modern shoes have soles made from natural rubber, polyurethane, or polyvinyl chloride (PVC) compounds. Soles can be a single material in a single layer or with multiple structures or layers and materials. When various layers are used, soles may consist of an insole, midsole, and an outsole.

Stacked Heel

This is a heel that has horizontal lines, indicating that it is made up of stacked layers of leather, or a heel with that appearance.

Suede

Suede is leather that has been sanded or roughed to produce a surface with a soft texture or "nap". Suede leather is made from the underside of the skin, primarily lamb, although goat, pig, calf, and deer are commonly used.

Throat

The throat is the main opening of a shoe extending from the vamp to the ankle.

Toe-box

This is a stiff piece of material placed inside the vamp to retain the dome-like shape over the toes. The toe-box can take many shapes, including flat, high, or wide. The toe-box is the part that covers and protects the toes. People with toe deformities, or individuals who experience toe swelling (such as long-distance runners) usually require a larger toe box.

Toe Thong Post

This is the part of a thong sandal that actually fits between the toes.

Tongue

A tongue is a strip of leather (or other material) sewn into the vamp of a laced shoe, and it extends to the throat of the shoe. The tongue sits on the top centre part of the shoe on top of the bridge of the foot. Tongues are found on any shoe with laces. The tongue also protects the top of the foot and prevents laces from rubbing against the foot.

Upper

This is simply the upper part of the shoe, not including the sole. Uppers may be made from leather, fabric or synthetics. The upper helps hold the shoe onto the foot. In the simplest cases, such as sandals or flip-flops, this may be nothing more than a few straps for holding the sole in place. Closed footwear, such as boots, and most men's shoes, will have a more complex upper. This part is often decorated or is made in a certain style to look attractive. The upper is connected to the sole by a strip of leather, rubber, or plastic that is stitched between it and the sole, known as a welt. Most uppers have a mechanism, such as laces, straps with buckles, zippers, elastic, Velcro straps, buttons, or snaps, for tightening the upper on the foot. Uppers with laces usually have a tongue that helps seal the laced opening and protect the foot from abrasion by the laces. Uppers with laces also have eyelets or hooks to make it easier to tighten and loosen the laces and to prevent the lace from tearing through the upper material.

Vamp

This is the front part of a shoe upper that covers the toes and part of the foot.

Welt

A strip of leather sewn between the insole and the outsole to create greater durability. The welt can be made to 'stick out' from the sole and further ornament the shoe.

Wing Tip (Also known as a Brogue)

A wing tip is a type of shoe with overlays and stitched, perforated trim, common in dress styles.

Visit www.henleypoint.ca

Henley Point Production

ABOUT THE AUTHOR

Photo: Experiencing The Vog Vault, Fluevog, 686 Queen Street West – Toronto. Formally a TD Bank vault.

Josée's experience spans teaching in Thailand and working with the Canadian military on Canada's east coast to paralegal work in Toronto and executive support in insurance and corporate regulation services. She has steered several corporate outreach and communications campaigns, and has been developing web design and digital conference production for several years. Fully bilingual (French and English), Josée is nearing completion of a diploma in Professional Communication at Toronto Metropolitan University. An avid reader, as well as a collector of custom fashions and vintage toys, Josée is the author of *One, Two, Buckle My Shoe Collection*. She lives in Toronto with her husband, Steven, and two cats, Sophie and Jules

ALSO BY JOSÉE SCALABRINI

ONE, TWO, BUCKLE MY SHOE COLLECTION
THE ULTIMATE GUIDE TO OUR SOLES
ISBN: 978-1-7778-3472-2

www.ingramcontent.com/pod-product-compliance
Lightning Source LLC
Chambersburg PA
CBHW061119170426
43209CB00013B/1613